1

Wonderful WORLD

SECOND EDITION

WORKBOOK

T0349559

NATIONAL GEOGRAPHIC
L E A R N I N G

Australia · Brazil · Mexico · Singapore · United Kingdom · United States

NATIONAL GEOGRAPHIC
LEARNING

***Wonderful World 1* Workbook, Second Edition**

Vice President, Editorial Director: John McHugh

Executive Editor: Siân Mavor

Commissioning Editor: Kayleigh Buller

Senior Development Editor: Karen Haller Beer

Head of Strategic Marketing EMEA ELT:
  Charlotte Ellis

Product Marketing Executive: Ellen Setterfield

Head of Production and Design: Celia Jones

Senior Content Project Manager: Phillipa
  Davidson-Blake

Manufacturing Manager: Eyvett Davis

Cover Design: Lisa Trager

Interior Design and Composition:
  Lumina Datamatics, Inc.

For product information and technology assistance, contact us at
Cengage Learning Customer & Sales Support, cengage.com/contact

For permission to use material from this text or product,
submit all requests online at **cengage.com/permissions**
Further permissions questions can be emailed to
permissionrequest@cengage.com

Workbook: Level 1
ISBN: 978-1-4737-6061-5

National Geographic Learning
Cheriton House, North Way
Andover, Hampshire, SP10 5BE
United Kingdom

National Geographic Learning, a Cengage Learning Company, has a mission to bring the world to the classroom and the classroom to life. With our English language programs, students learn about their world by experiencing it. Through our partnerships with National Geographic and TED Talks, they develop the language and skills they need to be successful global citizens and leaders.

Locate your local office at **international.cengage.com/region**

Visit National Geographic Learning online at **NGL.Cengage.com/ELT**
Visit our corporate website at **www.cengage.com**

Printed in Greece by BAKIS sa
Print Number: 07   Print Year: 2023

Contents

Alphabet

1 **Match.**

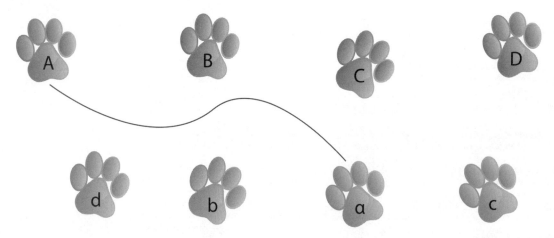

2 **Write *A*, *B*, *C* or *D*.**

__B_ OY

___ AMEL

___ NT

___ UCK

3 **Write and say.**

What's your name?

My name's

_____ .

4 Circle *e, f, g* and *h*.

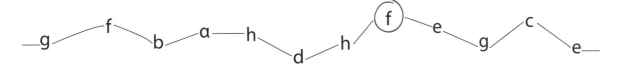

g   f   b   a   h   d   h   (f)   e   g   c   e

5 Find, circle and colour.

A G H A B
E C I B G
G E P E I
G D P C R
F R O G L

6 Colour. Write and say.

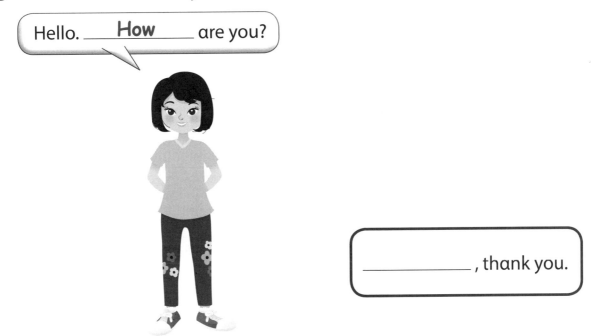

Hello. ____**How**____ are you?

_____ , thank you.

7 **Match.**

8 **Circle.**

9 **Write and say.**

What's your name?

My name's Sophie.

_____ are you?

Fine, _____ you.

10 Circle *m*, *n*, *o* and *p*.

11 Write M, N, O or P.

12 Join the dots. Write.

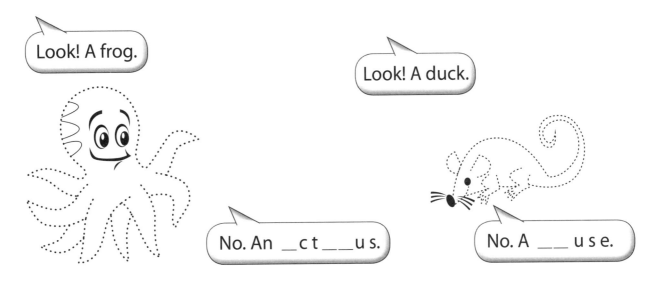

Look! A frog.

No. An __ c t ___ u s.

Look! A duck.

No. A ___ u s e.

13 **Match.**

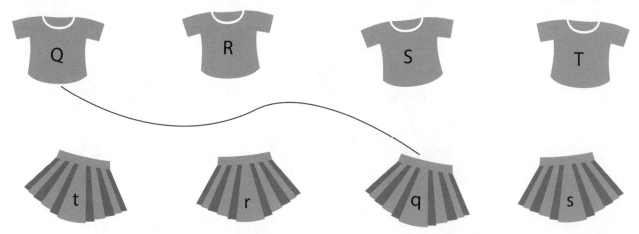

14 **Circle.**

pitigerquosunnigqueenderrobotlt

15 **Join the dots. Read and colour.**

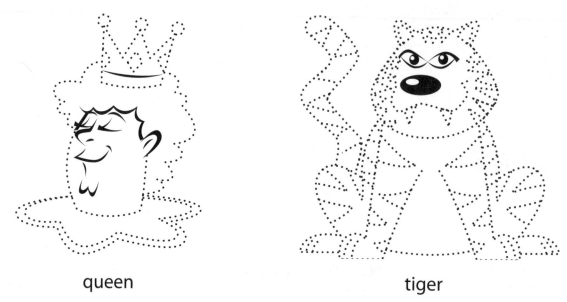

queen   tiger

16 Write.

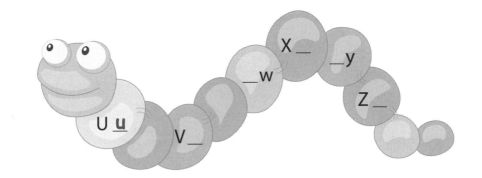

U u

V __

__w

X __

__y

Z __

17 Find, circle and colour.

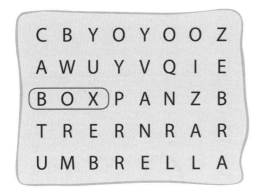

C B Y O Y O O Z
A W U Y V Q I E
(B O X) P A N Z B
T R E R N R A R
U M B R E L L A

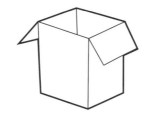

18 Colour and say.

Goodbye!

Thank you!

Bye!

You're welcome!

19 Write.

A <u>B</u> C _ _ _ F _ H I _ _ _ L M _ O _ _ _ R S _ _ V _ X _ Z

_ b _ d e _ g _ _ j k _ _ _ n _ p q _ _ _ t u _ w _ y _

20 Write and say.

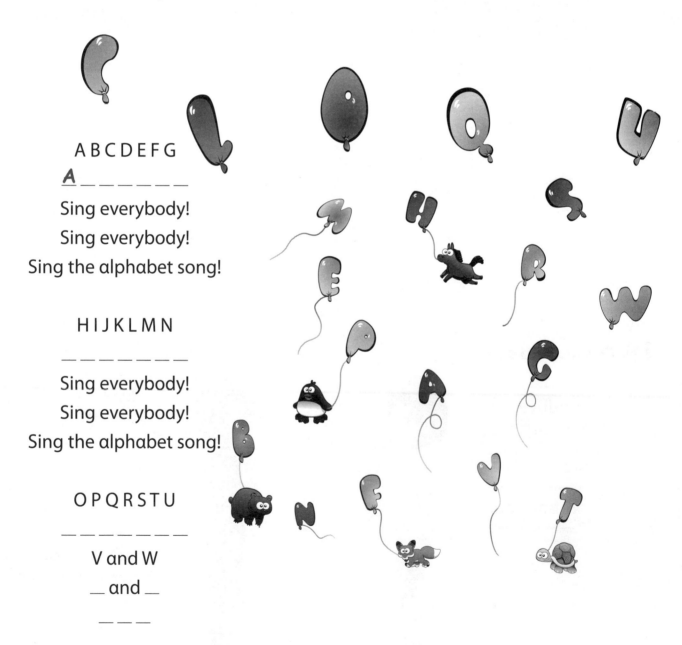

A B C D E F G

<u>A</u> _ _ _ _ _ _

Sing everybody!
Sing everybody!
Sing the alphabet song!

H I J K L M N

_ _ _ _ _ _ _

Sing everybody!
Sing everybody!
Sing the alphabet song!

O P Q R S T U

_ _ _ _ _ _ _

V and W

_ and _

_ _ _

Colours

1 **Colour and say.**

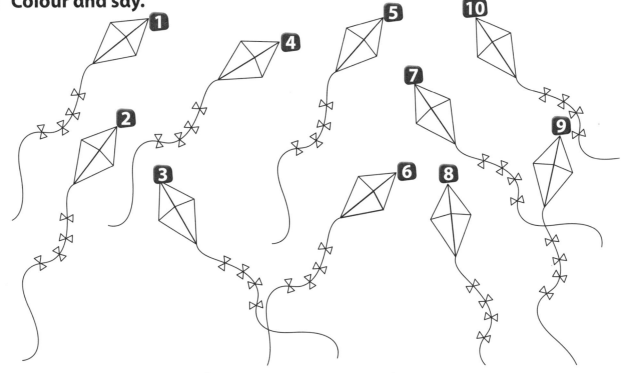

1 blue	5 white	8 red	
2 pink	6 black	9 orange	
3 yellow	7 green	10 brown	
4 purple			

2 **Write and colour.**

1 w <u>h i t e</u> 　　　　2 g _ _ e _ 　　　　3 y e _ _ _ _ _

4 p _ _ k 　　5 b _ _ w _ 　　6 _ e _ 　　7 _ l _ e

8 p _ _ p _ _ 　　9 _ r _ n _ e 　　10 _ l _ c k

Numbers

1 Circle and write.

onemitwodthreefhpfourqgfiveksixtussevenxeightjznineatenrtye

_____one_____   _____

_____   _____

_____   _____

_____   _____

_____   _____

2 Match.

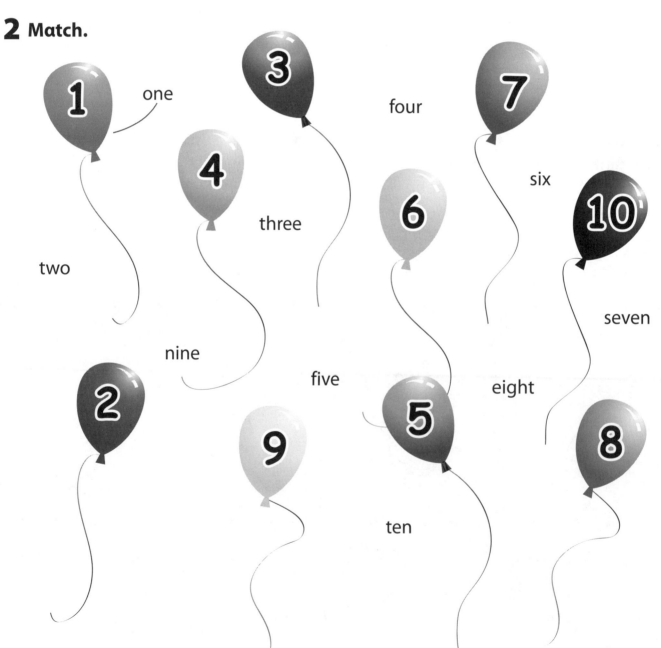

one

three

two

nine

five

four

six

seven

eight

ten

Greetings

1 **Write.**

 A _l_ e _x_

 A _ a

 _ o m a _

 _ o p h i _

2 **Match and write.**

What's your name?

How old are you?

How are you?

Fine, thanks.

My name's _____.

I'm _____.

3 **Draw.**

_____

you!

1 My Family

Lesson 1

1 Circle.

1

baby / mum

3

mum / dad

5

brother / sister

2

mum / brother

4

dad / sister

2 Read. Draw and colour.

This is my family.

I have a mum, a dad, a big brother and a baby sister.

I am ten years old!

3 Write.

baby~~ ~~ant~~ mum insect dad hippo
egg mouse octopus sister

a
baby
_____
_____
_____
_____
_____

an
ant
_____
_____
_____
_____

4 Join the dots. Write and colour.

1

sun

3

_____

5

_____

2

_____

4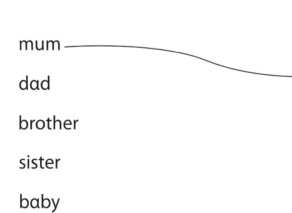

_____

5 Match and say.

mum

dad

brother

sister

baby

1 Match.

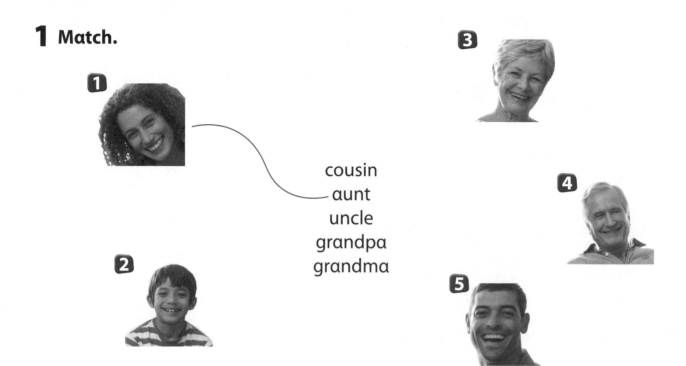

cousin
aunt
uncle
grandpa
grandma

2 Find, circle and write.

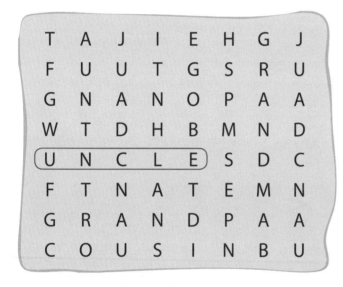

T	A	J	I	E	H	G	J
F	U	U	T	G	S	R	U
G	N	A	N	O	P	A	A
W	T	D	H	B	M	N	D
U	N	C	L	E	S	D	C
F	T	N	A	T	E	M	N
G	R	A	N	D	P	A	A
C	O	U	S	I	N	B	U

1

_____

4

_____

2

_____

5

uncle

3

_____

3 Circle.

1 My cousin **is** / **are** three years old.

2 You **am** / **are** my brother.

3 My grandma **are** / **is** great.

4 My uncle **am** / **is** cool!

5 My aunt **are** / **is** cool, too!

6 I **am** / **is** nine years old.

4 Write *'m, 're* or *'s.*

1 I ___'m___ a girl.

2 He _____ my grandpa.

3 My uncle _____ great.

4 You _____ eight years old.

5 She _____ my cousin.

6 I _____ cool!

5 Read and sing!

My f _ m i l y is cool
My _ _ m _ l _ is great.

So come on and celebrate!

Mum is g _ e _ t.
Dad is _ r _ _ t.
B _ _ t _ _ rs and _ i _ _ er _.
Yeah, they're gr _ _ t.

So come on and celebrate!

Lesson 3

1 Match.

1

3

4

funny

young

old

tall

short

2

5

2 Circle.

v c a young y p o funny l o o l d e s t s h o r t e w a t a l l l o

3 Write.

1 We are funny!   <u>We're</u> funny!

2 They are young.   _____ young.

3 You are great!   _____ great!

4 We are eight years old.   _____ eight years old.

5 You are tall.   _____ tall.

6 They are short.   _____ short.

4 Match and write.

> My grandpa is old   We're sisters   We're short
> You're my grandma   ~~They're funny!~~

<u>They're funny!</u>

_____

_____

_____

_____

5 Write and say.

> am   from   ~~name~~   years

Hi ! My __<u>name</u>__ is Zina. I _____ seven _____ old.
I am _____ Africa.

2 My School

Lesson 1

1 Write.

1 <u>c</u> l <u>a</u> ssr <u>o</u> <u>o</u> m

2 h ___ m ___ w ___ r ___

3 l ___ s ___ o ___

4 st ___ d ___ nt

5 t ___ a ___ h ___ r

2 Match.

1 It's his homework.

2 They're the students.

3 Andy and Leah are teachers.

4 It's a lesson.

3 Circle.

1 My **teacher** / **teachers** is funny!

2 Look! Five **classroom** / **classrooms**.

3 The **student** / **students** are tall.

4 The boys are in the **lesson** / **lessons**.

5 They are **sister** /**sisters**.

4 Circle and colour.

1 **one** / **three** hippos

2 **one** / **two** yo-yos

3 **one** / **four** egg

4 **one** / **five** camels

5 Read and say.

SOUNDS OF ENGLISH

homewor**k**

cousin

It's my **c**ousin. It's her homewor**k**.

Lesson 2

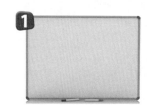
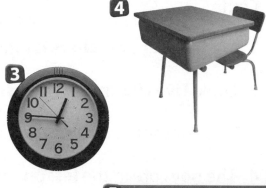

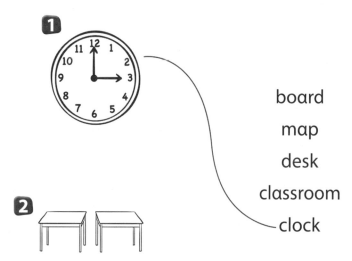

1 Write.

1 b _o_ _a_ rd

2 ___ h ___ i ___

3 clo ___ ___

4 d ___ s ___

5 ___ a ___

2 Match.

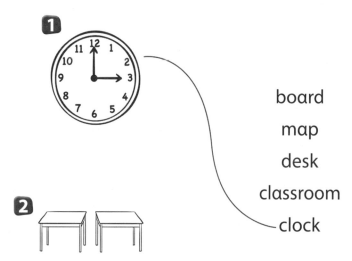

board

map

desk

classroom

clock

3 Order and write.

1 you / tall / aren't   You aren't tall.

2 a / isn't / map / it   _____

3 chairs / aren't / big / they _____

4 aren't / girls / we   _____

5 isn't / he / short   _____

4 Look. Tick (✓) or cross (✗).

1 It isn't a chair.   ☑

2 They aren't desks. ☐

3 He isn't short. ☐

4 They aren't students. 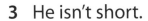 ☐

5 She isn't a teacher. ☐

5 Read and colour.

1 It's a yo-yo.
It isn't red. It's green.

2 They're zebras.
They aren't brown.
They're black and white.

3 It's a van.
It isn't yellow. It's blue.

4 It's an octopus.
It isn't blue. It's green
and purple.

 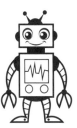 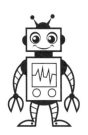

5 They're robots.
They aren't pink. They're red.

Lesson 3

1 Match

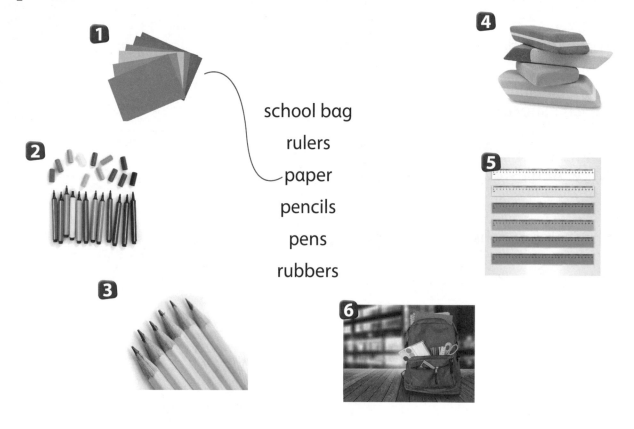

school bag

rulers

paper

pencils

pens

rubbers

2 Write.

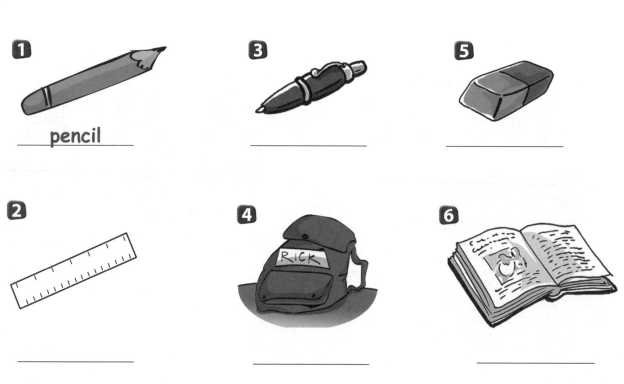

1. pencil

2. _____

3. _____

4. _____

5. _____

6. _____

3 Circle.

1 Is it a map?
(Yes, it is.) / No, it isn't.

2 Are they pens?
Yes, they are. /
No, they aren't.

3 Is it a ruler?
Yes, it is. / No, it isn't.

4 Is it a clock?
Yes, it is. / No, it isn't.

5 Are they books?
Yes, they are. /
No, they aren't.

4 Write and colour.

1 ___**Are**___ they red pencils? Yes, they ___**are**___ .

2 _____ the book blue? No, it _____ It's yellow.

3 _____ they brown chairs? Yes, they _____ .

4 _____ they orange rubbers? No, they _____ purple.

5 _____ the school bag orange? Yes, it _____ .

5 Read and say.

Look! It's my classroom. He's my teacher. His name is Mr Baker.

Yes, he is!

Is he funny?

1 Find, circle and write.

```
N R T E A C H E R U Z
T S I S T E R C L O C
P E D G N V T E A C H
A L A J B R O T H E R
F G D I L Y R B O A R
S T U D E N T C H A I
X Z W L E S S O N W M
P E F C M L R B O O U
B A C L A S S R O O M
```

Family

mum _____   _____

_____   _____

School

_____   _____

_____   _____

2 Circle and write.

1

a / ⓐn apple

3

a / an _____

5

a / an _____

2

a / an _____

4

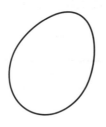

a / an _____

6

a / an _____

3 Tick (✔) or cross (✘).

1 The teacher is in the classroom. ✔
2 There are five desks. ☐
3 There are three books on the desk. ☐
4 There's one pen. ☐
5 There are three students. ☐

4 Write.

1 Are you short? __Yes, I am__ .

2 Is she cool? No, _____ .

3 Are they cousins? Yes,

_____ .

4 Are we best friends? Yes,

_____ .

5 Is it a classroom? No, _____ .

6 Is he funny? No, _____ .

5 Match.

She is my mum. She is nice.   He is my dad. He is tall.
~~They are my brothers. They are cool!~~

1 __They are my brothers. They are cool!__

2 _____

_____

3 _____

_____

3 Animals

Lesson 1

1 Write.

2 Read and colour.

1 four black cats

3 two green frogs

2 three grey rabbits

4 six orange and green fish

5 five blue birds

3 Circle.

1 (**This is**) / **That's** my sister.

3 **This is** / **That's** a mouse.

2 **This is** / **That's** a hippo.

4 **This is** / **That's** an egg.

4 Match and colour.

That's a zebra.   This is a yo-yo.   ~~That's an octopus.~~   This is a robot.

1

That's an octopus.

3

_____

2

_____

4

_____

5 Write and say.

The c __ t plays with the p __ per!

1 Match.

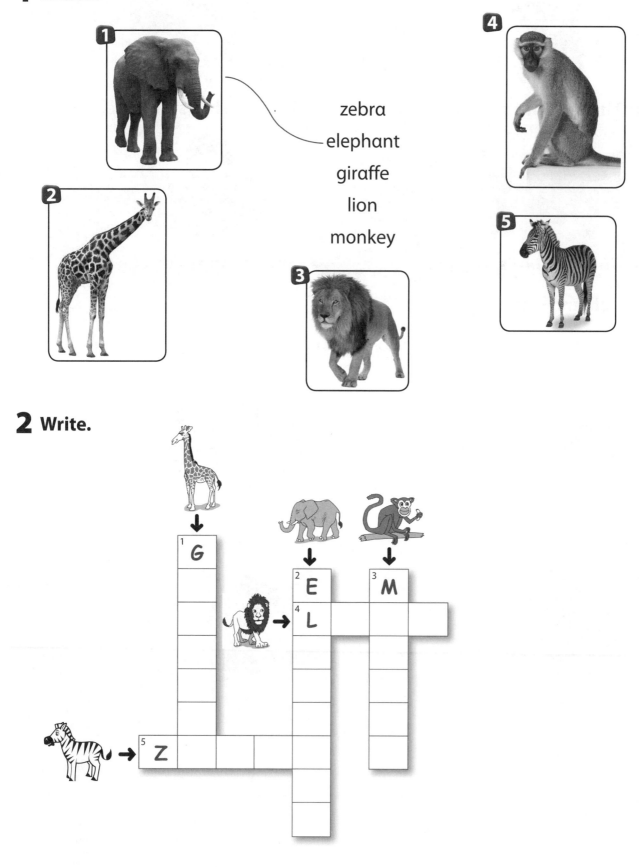

zebra
elephant
giraffe
lion
monkey

2 Write.

3 Circle.

1 (These) / **Those** are lions.

2 **These** / **Those** are elephants.

3 **These** / **Those** are monkeys.

4 **These** / **Those** are zebras.

5 **These** / **Those** are giraffes.

4 Order and write. Then say.

1 cats / are / my / these / black

<u>These are my black cats.</u>

2 baby / those / monkeys / are

3 these / are / lions / old

4 are / elephants / grey / those

5 Write. Then sing!

These are l <u>i o n s</u> – roar, roar!

Those are lions – r __ __ r, roar!

These are lions, those are lions,
roar, roar, roar!

These are m __ nke __ s – ooh, ooh!

Those are monkeys – ooh, ooh!

Th __ se are monkeys, those are
monkeys, ooh, ooh, ooh!

These are __ l e __ h __ nts— baraah!

Those are elephants— baraah!

These are elephants, th __ se are
elephants— baraaaah! Hurrrah!

Lesson 3

1 Circle.

lop(dolphin)cssharkfrtypenguinwatwhalebivspturtleeseaap

2 Join the dots. Write.

1 shark

2 _____

3 _____

4 _____

5 _____

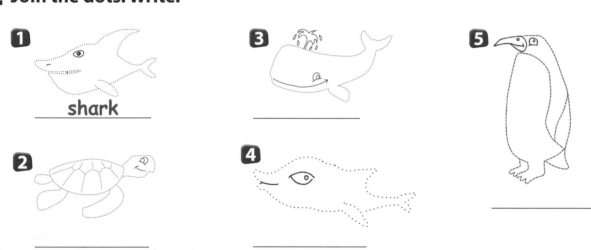

3 Match.

What are those?

What are these?

What's this?

What's that?

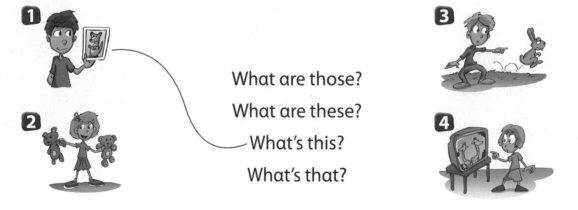

4 Circle and write.

1

What's **this** / **that?**

__It's__ a bird.

2

What are **there** / **those?**

_____ animals.

3

What's **this** / **that?**

_____ a giraffe.

4

What are **these** / **those?**

_____ turtles.

5 Write and say.

1

What's this?

It's ___a dolphin___ .

4

What's this?

It's _____ .

2

What's this?

It's _____ .

5

What's this?

It's _____ .

3

What's this?

It's _____ .

6

What's this?

It's _____ .

4 My House

Lesson 1

1 Write.

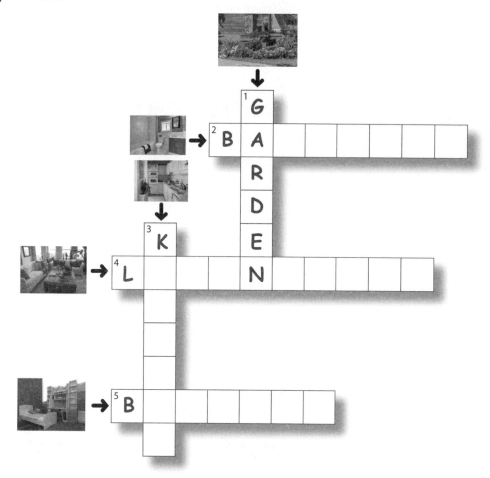

2 Match.

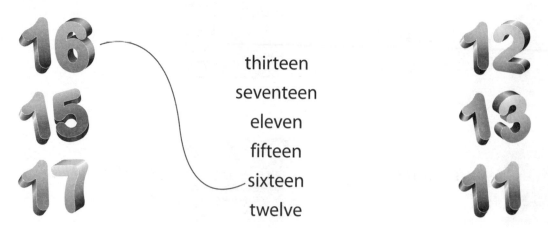

thirteen

seventeen

eleven

fifteen

sixteen

twelve

3 Circle.

1 **There's / There are** two classrooms.

2 **There's / There are** nineteen students.

3 **There's / There are** a cat in the living room.

4 **There's / There are** a nice kitchen, too!

5 **There's / There are** four bedrooms.

6 **There's / There are** a nest in the garden.

4 Write *There's* or *There are*.

1 _____There's_____ a nice kitchen.

2 _____ three bedrooms.

3 _____ two bathrooms.

4 _____ three birds and a rabbit in the garden.

5 _____ a living room. It is grey and yellow!

5 Read and colour.

There's a school bag on the chair.

There are two girls in the kitchen.

Lesson 2

1 Circle.

bed / (TV)

toy / computer

lamp / book

bed / toy

lamp / computer

TV / book

2 Look. Write the number.

1	bed	5
2	computer	
3	lamp	
4	TV	
5	book	

3 Circle.

1 There **aren't** / **is** any toys in the living room.

2 There **is** / **are** a lamp in your house.

3 There **isn't** / **aren't** a bed in the bathroom.

4 There **is** / **are** books on my desk.

5 There **isn't** / **aren't** a bath in the bedroom.

4 Write *are, aren't, is, isn't.*

1 __Are__ and there any birds in the garden? No, there __aren't__.

2 _____ the computer in the living room? Yes, it _____.

3 _____ there any toys in the bedroom? Yes, there _____.

4 _____ my book in the kitchen? No, it _____.

5 _____ there any lamps in your house? No, there _____.

5 Read and draw.

My bedroom has yellow walls. I have a bed and a desk. There are two books on the desk and a lamp. There aren't any toys in my room, but there is a computer.

1 Match.

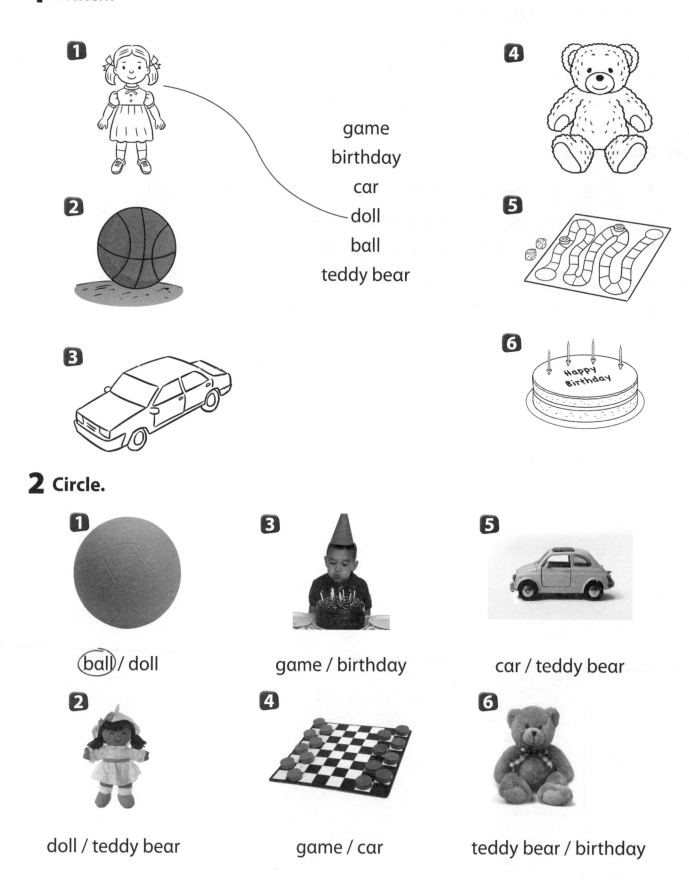

game
birthday
car
doll
ball
teddy bear

2 Circle.

1. ball / doll

2. doll / teddy bear

3. game / birthday

4. game / car

5. car / teddy bear

6. teddy bear / birthday

3 Circle.

1 There's **the** / a doll on the chair.

2 There is **a** / **an** game in the living room.

3 Look! **The** / **An** octopus! The octopus is orange and white.

4 I've got **a** / **an** ball and a teddy bear. **The** / **A** teddy bear is on the bed.

5 Is there a computer in the kitchen? No, there isn't. **The** / **A** computer is in the bedroom.

4 Write *a, an* or *the*.

It's my birthday today. It's my friend's birthday, too. We're eight years old today!

There are friends at my house. We're in (1) _____ living room.
There are lots of toys! There's (2) _____ nice teddy bear. There's
(3) _____ doll, too! There's (4) _____ ball for my friend. There's (5) _____
cool game for me! There are two cars. (6) _____ red one is for my friend.
There is (7) _____ orange car for me. What a great birthday!

5 Write and draw. Then say.

1

look / pencil / green
<u>Look! A pencil.</u>
<u>The pencil is green.</u>

3

look / ball / red
_____
_____

2

look / teddy bear / brown
_____
_____

4

look / car / yellow
_____
_____

1 Find, circle and write.

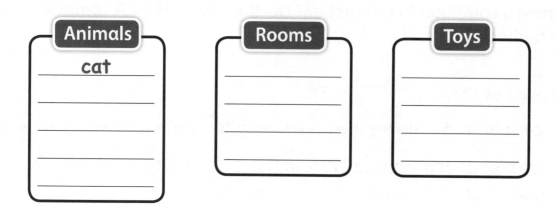

cat fish bird dog rabbit game car garden
bathroom bedroom doll ball kitchen

Animals
cat
_____
_____
_____
_____

Rooms
_____
_____
_____
_____

Toys
_____
_____
_____
_____

2 Circle.

1   What are those? **It's / (They're)** lamps.

2   What are these? **It's / They're** teddy bears.

3   What's this? **It's / They're** a bed.

4   What's that? **It's / They're** a birthday cake.

5   What are these? **It's / They're** penguins.

6   What's this? **It's / They're** a whale.

3 Write.

Are there   Is there   There are   There aren't   ~~There's~~   There isn't

1 Look! __There's__ a dolphin!

2 _____ any toys.

3 _____ any zebras? No, there aren't.

4 _____ eleven bedrooms!

5 _____ a monkey in the tree? Yes, there is.

6 _____ a game. There's a doll.

4 Match and write.

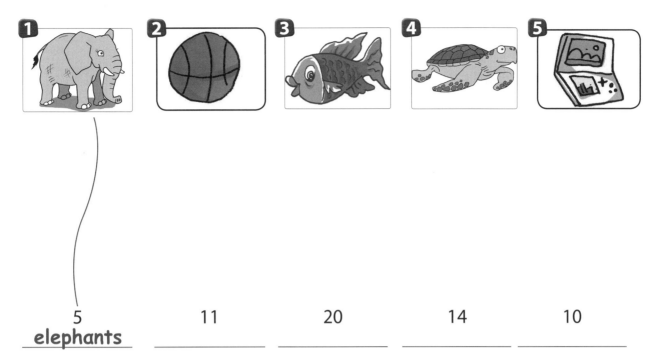

5	11	20	14	10
elephants				

5 Look again! Write.

1 There ___are___ ___five___ elephants.

2 There _____ _____ computers.

3 There _____ _____ balls.

4 There _____ _____ fish.

5 There _____ _____ turtles.

5 My Body

Lesson 1

1 **Match.**

1 head

2 arms

3 hands

4 legs

5 feet

2 **Find, circle and write.**

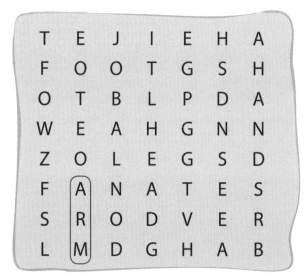

T	E	J	I	E	H	A
F	O	O	T	G	S	H
O	T	B	L	P	D	A
W	E	E	A	H	G	N	N
Z	O	L	E	G	S	D
F	A	N	A	T	E	S
S	R	O	D	V	E	R
L	M	D	G	H	A	B

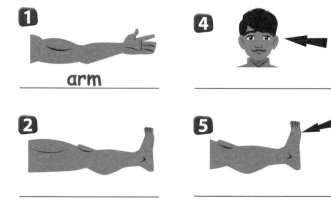

1

_____arm_____

2

_____

3

_____

4

_____

5

_____

3 Write.

He's got   ~~It's got~~   I've got   She's got   You've got

1 __It's got__ four legs.

2 _____ two teddy bears.

3 _____ a nice computer.

4 _____ a big robot.

5 _____ three books.

4 Write.

1 I have got one head.   __I've got__ one head.

2 It has got black feet!   _____ black feet!

3 They have got green legs.   _____ green legs.

4 You have got a big house!   _____ a big house!

5 She has got one sister.   _____ one sister.

5 Read and colour.

The robot has one red head. It has two green eyes. It has four black feet. It has four yellow legs! It has six orange arms. It has six purple hands.

1 Circle.

apo eyes refdearsmoonosexihairemasmmouthirsfaceeopaintt

2 Write.

1

eyes

2

_____

3

_____

4

_____

5

_____

7

_____

3 Circle.

1 He **has** / (**hasn't**) got paint on his face

2 The doll **has** / **hasn't** got two eyes.

3 They **have** / **haven't** got a cat.

4 They **have** / **haven't** got long hair.

5 It **has** / **hasn't** got eight legs.

4 Read and say.

I've got a trunk for a nose.
I've got big ears.
I haven't got any hands.
Do you know what I am?
Do you know what I am?
I'm an elephant! That's what I am.

I've got four legs.
I've got black and white stripes.
I haven't got any arms.
Do you know what I am?
Do you know what I am?
I'm a zebra! That's what I am.

5 Look again! Draw the animals in Activity 4.

Lesson 3

1 **Match.**

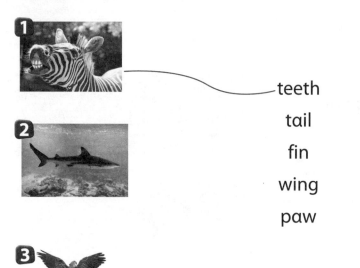

teeth

tail

fin

wing

paw

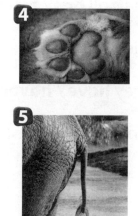

2 **Circle.**

1 teeth

2 tail

3 fin

4 wing

5 paw

3 Write and say.

1   <u>How many</u> wings <u>has</u> a bird got?
    It's got two wings.

2   How many _____ _____ a dog got?
    It's got one tail.

3   How many paws has a cat got?
    _____ _____ four _____ .

4   How many fins _____ a shark _____?
    It's got one fin.

5   _____ teeth _____ a rabbit got?
    It's got 28 teeth.

4 Circle.

1   Snakes **have** / (**haven't**) got one eye.   4   Lions **have** / **haven't** got four paws.

2   A frog **has** / **hasn't** got a tail.   5   A hippo **has** / **hasn't** got wings.

3   A dolphin **has** / **hasn't** got a fin.   6   Dogs **have** / **haven't** got three legs.

5 Read and draw.

This is a monster. It's got one head.

How many eyes has it got?

It's got five eyes.

Has it got arms?

It's got three arms.

How many teeth has it got?

It's got ten teeth.

Has it got a tail?

It's got two tails.

6 My Clothes

Lesson 1

1 Match.

1 trousers [a]

2 T-shirt [ ]

3 shoes [ ]

4 socks [ ]

5 skirt [ ]

2 Write.

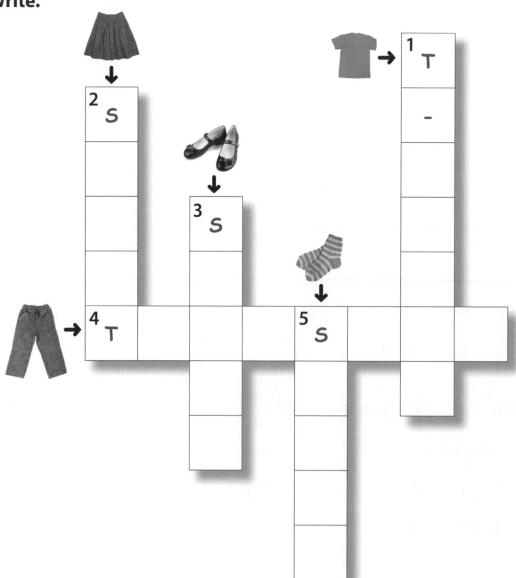

3 Read and say. Colour.

1 She's got a pink and blue T-shirt.

3 His socks are orange.

2 They've got blue trousers.

4 I've got a purple skirt.

4 Circle.

1 They've got new shoes. **Their** / **Our** shoes are cool!

2 I've got a nice skirt. **Her** / **My** skirt is yellow.

3 We've got lots of toys. We love **our** / **your** cars!

4 I'm John. What's **their** / **your** name?

5 Peter has got a book in **her** / **his** bag.

6 Anna's got blue trousers. **Its** / **Her** T-shirt is blue too.

5 Write and say.

1 _____My_____ name's Jalita. My jeans are blue.

2 Isla has got a teddy bear. _____ got green shoes.

3 Your T-shirt is black and _____ trousers are black too.

4 They're brothers. _____ socks are red and cool!

5 That's Emma. _____ skirt is nice.

6 We're friends. _____ names are Andrew and Tony.

Lesson 2

1 Circle.

1 coat

3 boots

5 hat

2 dress

4 jumper

2 Write and colour.

1 <u>d</u> re <u>s</u> <u>s</u>

2 c ___ a ___

3 b ___ ___ t ___

4 h ___ ___

5 ___ u ___ ___ e ___

3 Order and write.

1 Lin / boots / warm
Lin's boots are warm.

2 the / girl / jumper / green
_____

3 the / boy / coat / white
_____

4 the / girl / dress / blue
_____

5 the / boy / socks / yellow
_____

4 Match and write.

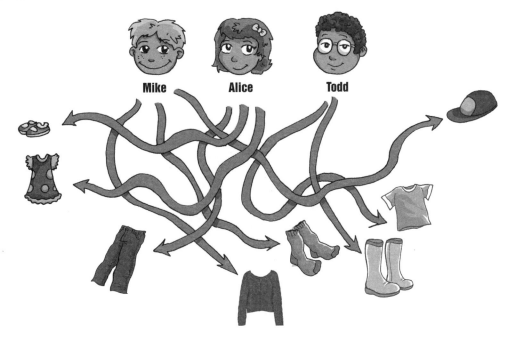

1 They're ___Todd's___ boots.

2 It's _____ hat.

3 It's _____ dress.

4 It's _____ jumper.

5 They're _____ shoes.

6 It's _____ T-shirt.

7 They're _____ trousers.

8 They're _____ socks.

5 Read and draw. Then say.

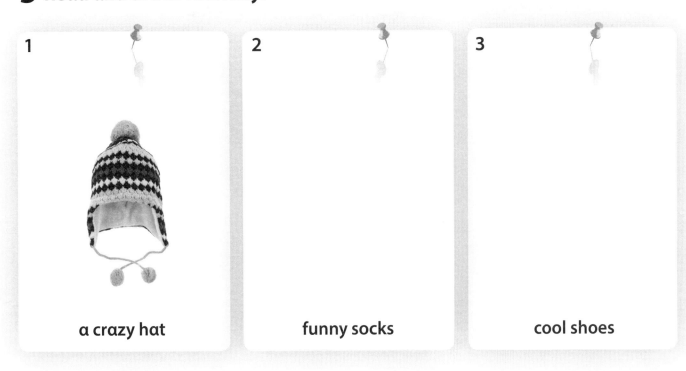

1 a crazy hat

2 funny socks

3 cool shoes

1 Circle.

nbc(big)loanewwtbrpriprettyinguglycvtltsmallyb

2 Match.

big
small
new
pretty
ugly

3 Write.

1 My _____new_____ _____hat_____ is green. (hat, new)

2 I've got _____ _____ . (warm, boots)

3 Mum's got a _____ _____ . (skirt, white)

4 She's got a _____ _____ in her bag. (dress, pretty)

5 We love our _____ _____ jumpers. (blue, new)

4 Write.

1 shoes / ugly / the / are

The shoes are ugly.

2 green/ is / this / my / jumper

_____

3 warm / she's / hat / got / a

_____

4 a / T-shirt / I've / new / got

_____

5 Read and draw. Then say.

My name's Carolina.
My trousers are blue.
My T-shirt is pink.
My hat is red and my
boots are black.
I'm cool!

1 Circle.

1 I've got a **new** / **old** baby rabbit called Sam.

2 My baby rabbit has got one **paw** / **tail**.

3 My baby rabbit is **small** / **big**.

4 Sam has got blue **eyes** / **legs**.

5 Sam lives in the **garden** / **bathroom**.

6 He's always **warm** / **cool**.

2 Write.

his	her	~~our~~	their	its

1 _____Our_____ dog is black and white.

2 _____ T-shirts are white.

3 _____ shorts are new.

4 _____ hair is long.

5 _____ tail is white.

3 Read and match.

1 They haven't got shoes on their feet.

2 He has got a hat on his head.

3 No, she hasn't got long hair.

4 Look! They've got a small cat with black fur.

5 Have you got a new coat? Yes, I have.

a

b

c

d

e

4 Circle.

1 Have you got shoes on your feet? Yes, I **have** / **haven't**.

2 Talita **has** / **hasn't** got a cat. She's got a fish.

3 He **has** / **hasn't** got a jumper. It's red.

4 Reynaldo and Josef **have** / **haven't** got new T-shirts. They've got new jumpers.

5 Has she got a yellow dress? No, she **has** / **hasn't**.

5 Order and write.

1 coat / black / is / Ming's _____Ming's coat is black._____

2 jumper / old / is / Mum's _____

3 big / the / dog's / ears / are _____

4 Tai's / pretty / dress / is _____

7 What Can You Do?

Lesson 1

1 Circle.

swim / (cook)

write / listen to music

read / speak English

read / listen to music

cook / speak English

write / swim

2 Write. Then draw.

cook   listen to music   read   write   speak   ~~swim~~

They can ___swim___ .

He can _____ .

He can _____ .

She can _____ .

She can _____ .

I can _____ English.

3 Match.

1 Grandma can cook. `d`

2 The girl can read. ☐

3 Whales can swim. ☐

4 The students can speak English. ☐

5 The friends can write. ☐

a  d

b  e

c

4 Look and write.

1 I can  ____**read**____ and  _____ .

2 I can _____ and  _____ .

3 I can _____ and  _____ .

5 Write and say.

Dance everybody! We can dance.

Dance everybody! We can d <u>a</u> n <u>c</u> e.

Sit down, stand up.

We can cook!

Sit down, s __ __ n __ up.

We can c __ __ k !

Read and write, r __ __ d and

    w __ i __ e.

You c _ n speak English, too!

Read and write, read and write.

You __ a __ s __ e __ k English, too!

1 Match.

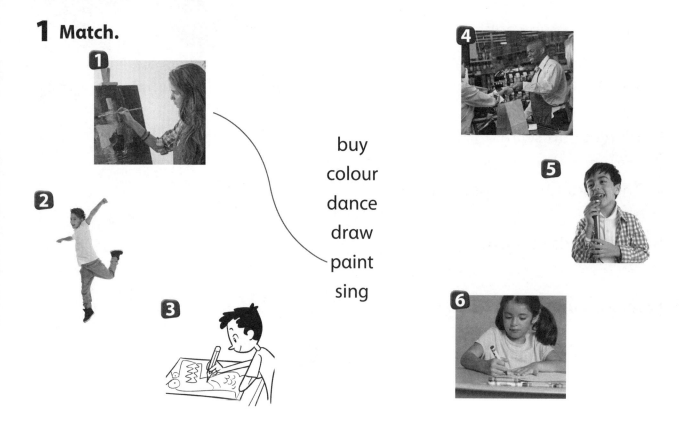

buy
colour
dance
draw
paint
sing

2 Circle.

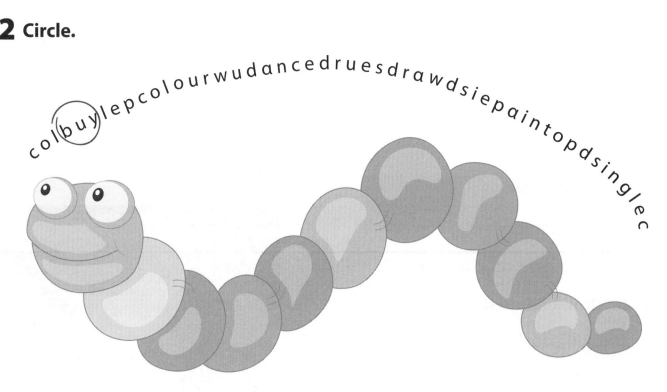

colbuylepcolourwudancedruesdrawdsiepaintopdsinglec

3 Circle.

1 He's a baby. He **can** / **(can't)** read.

2 Bill **can** / **can't** write. He hasn't got a pen.

3 Zebras **can** / **can't** run.

4 Oh no! Tina **can** / **can't** dance!

5 Dolphins **can** / **can't** swim.

6 My brother's cool. He **can** / **can't** sing well.

4 Write.

Jane	✗	✗	✗	✔
Rick	✗	✔	✔	✔

1 Rick _____can_____ dance.

2 Jane _____ dance.

3 Jane and Rick _____ draw.

4 Rick _____ paint.

5 Jane _____ paint.

6 Jane and Rick _____ sing.

5 Read. Tick (✔) or cross (✗).

Tom can swim. He can't dance.

He can sing and he can draw.

He can't paint but he can colour.

colour	dance	draw	paint	sing	swim
					✔

1 Join the dots and write.

1    **2**   **3**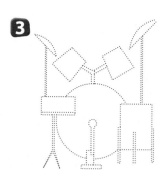

<u>play the recorder</u>   _____   _____

2 Write.

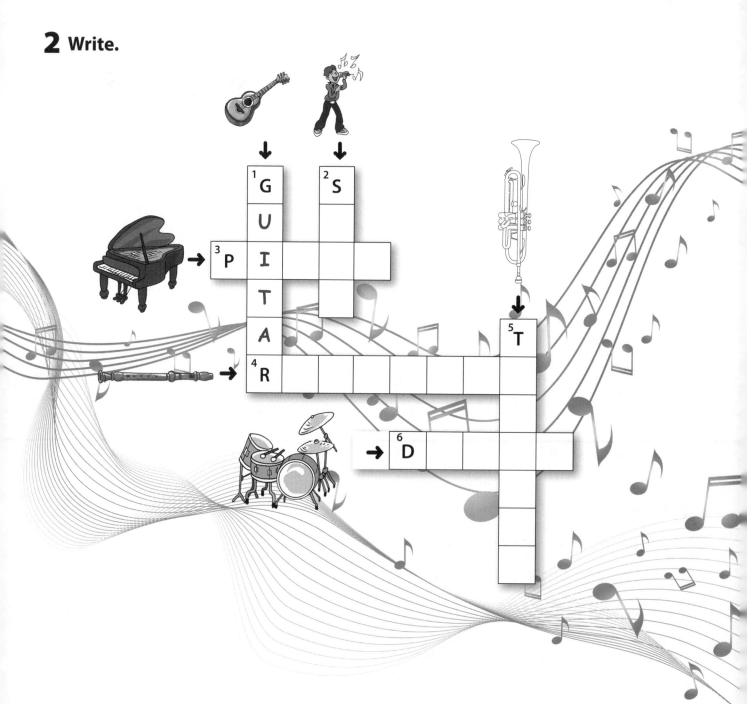

3 Match.

1 Can Phil play the guitar? ——————— **a** Yes, he can.

2 Can Natalie sing? **b** No, she can't.

3 Can Alice swim? **c** Yes, she can.

4  Can Mike and Joe dance? **d** Yes, they can.

4 Write about you.

1 Can you swim? _Yes, I can._

2 Can you play the drums? _____

3 Can you draw? _____

4 Can you sing? _____

5 Can you play the recorder? _____

6 Can you play the piano? _____

5 Read and match.

1 She can read. ☐ c

2 He can play the drums. ☐

3 She can sing. ☐

4 She can't play the guitar. ☐

5 He can listen to music. ☐

6 She can play the piano. ☐

8 Let's Play!

Lesson 1

1 Match.

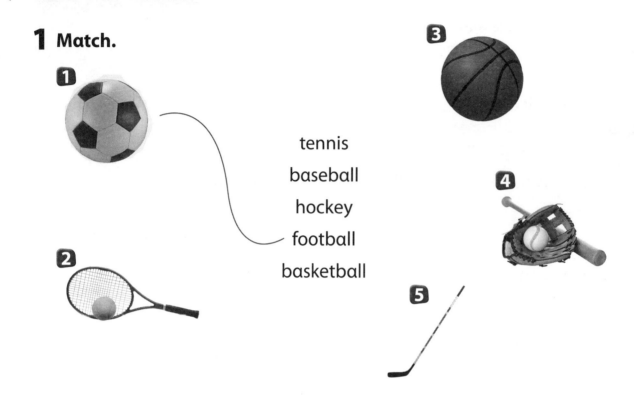

tennis
baseball
hockey
football
basketball

2 Find, circle and write.

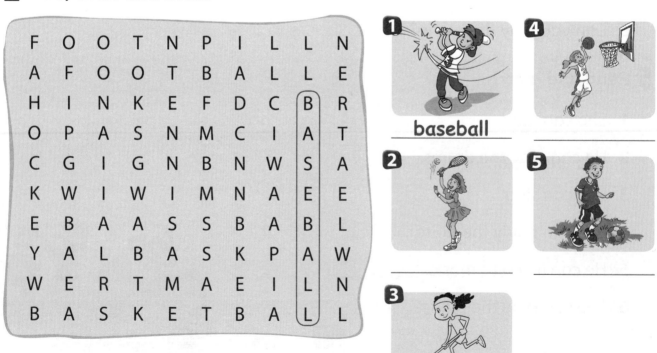

F	O	O	T	N	P	I	L	L	N
A	F	O	O	T	B	A	L	L	E
H	I	N	K	E	F	D	C	B	R
O	P	A	S	N	M	C	I	A	T
C	G	I	G	N	B	N	W	S	A
K	W	I	W	I	M	N	A	E	E
E	B	A	A	S	S	B	A	B	L
Y	A	L	B	A	S	K	P	A	W
W	E	R	T	M	A	E	I	L	N
B	A	S	K	E	T	B	A	L	L

1. baseball

2. _____

3. _____

4. _____

5. _____

3 Write.

They're playing basketball.   ~~They're playing football.~~   We're playing tennis.   I'm playing the drums.   You're playing the piano.   She's singing.

1. They're playing football.

2. _____

3. _____

4. _____

5. _____

6. _____

4 Write.

1 They are reading.
   They're reading.

2 We are playing football.
   _____

3 You are cooking in the kitchen.
   _____

4 We are singing a song.
   _____

5 They are listening to music.
   _____

6 You are playing the drums.
   _____

Lesson 2

1 **Look and write.**

catch   hit   ~~jump~~   kick   run   throw

1

jump

3

_____

5

_____

2

_____

4

_____

6

_____

2 **Look and match.**

1   He is jumping.

2   He is catching the ball.

3   He is throwing the ball.

4   He is hitting the ball with his hand.

5   He is kicking the ball with his foot.

a

b

c

d

e

3 Circle.

1 **I'm** / **aren't** listening to music.

2 My friends **isn't** / **aren't** playing baseball.

3 He **isn't** / **aren't** jumping. He's running.

4 They **isn't** / **aren't** playing hockey.

5 You **isn't** / **aren't** throwing the ball!

6 She **isn't** / **aren't** swimming today.

4 Look. Tick (✔) or cross (✗).

1 The dolphin isn't swimming. ✗

2 They aren't painting. ☐

3 He isn't kicking the ball. ☐

4 She isn't throwing the ball. ☐

5 We aren't playing hockey. ☐

5 Read, draw and say.

I'm not playing football.
I'm playing basketball.

We're playing tennis.
We aren't playing
baseball.

He isn't jumping.
He's running.

1 **Circle.**

match / watch

lose / win

match / team

win / watch

lose / win

2 **Look and write.**

Lisa   Tom   Penny   Anna   Paula   Harry

1   He isn't jumping. He's running.   It's Tom.

2   She isn't cooking. She's playing the guitar.   _____

3   She isn't playing tennis. She's reading a book.   _____

4   He isn't playing the guitar. He's swimming.   _____

5   She isn't kicking a ball. She's cooking.   _____

6   She isn't swimming. She's playing tennis.   _____

3 Match.

1 Are you playing the drums?
2 Is Timothy throwing the ball?
3 Is the dog running?
4 Are we playing basketball?
5 Are the boys playing hockey?
6 Is she winning the match?

a Yes, we are.
b No, I'm not.
c No, it isn't.
d Yes, he is.
e Yes, she is.
f No, they aren't.

4 Circle.

1 Is Dad cooking?
2 Is Mum playing a game?
3 Are Joe and Lily throwing a ball?
4 Is Dan playing the drums.
5 Is the dog jumping?
6 Is the cat jumping?

(Yes, he is.) / No, he isn't.
Yes, she is. / No, she isn't.
Yes, they are. / No, they aren't.
Yes, he is. / No, he isn't.
Yes, it is. / No, it isn't.
Yes, it is. / No, it isn't.

5 Look again. Write.

1 Mum __isn't playing__ a game. She __'s reading__ a book.

2 Dan _____ a guitar. He _____ the drums.

3 Are Joe and Lily _____ a ball? Yes, they _____ .

4 _____ Dad _____ football? No, he _____ . He _____ .

67

1 Write.

1 Are they reading?   Yes, they are.

2 Are they jumping?   _____

3 Are they playing football?   _____

4 Are they dancing?   _____

5 Are they listening to music? _____

6 Are they throwing a ball?   _____

7 Are they running?   _____

8 Are they playing the piano? _____

2 Write about you.

1 Can you read?   Yes, I can.

2 Can you swim?   _____

3 Can you play a trumpet?   _____

4 Can you kick a ball?   _____

5 Can you cook?   _____

3 Write.

1 (she / play) <u>Can you play the piano?</u> (✔) <u>Yes, I can.</u>

2 (she / swim) _____ (✗) _____

3 (he / hit) _____ (✔) _____

4 (they / play) _____ (✗) _____

5 (you / play) _____ (✗) _____

4 Match.

1 Are you playing football?   a. No, he isn't.

2 Are they running?   b. Yes, she is.

3 Is he cooking in the kitchen?   c. No, I'm not.

4 Is she buying shoes in the market? d. No, we aren't.

5 Is the shark swimming?   e. Yes, they are.

6 Are we losing the match?   f. Yes, it is.

5 Write and draw. Say.

My name is _____ .

I can _____ and _____ .

I can't _____ .

9 My Town

Lesson 1

1 Look. Write the number.

1 cinema   **d**

2 theatre   ☐

3 museum   ☐

4 library   ☐

5 zoo   ☐

2 Read and match.

1 I'm going to the zoo.

2 I'm going to the museum.

3 I'm going to the library.

4 I'm going to the cinema.

5 We're going to the theatre.

a

b

c

d

e

3 Match.

1 What is Mary doing?

2 What is John doing?

3 Where is Mum going?

4 Where are Jane and Annie going?

5 What are Paul and James doing?

6 Where are you going?

a He's playing football.

b They're going to the cinema.

c She's watching a tennis match.

d I'm going to the library.

e She's going to the theatre.

f They're playing the drums.

4 Write.

> What are they doing?   ~~What are you doing?~~   What is it doing?
> Where is she going?   Where are they going?   Where are you going?

What are you doing?
I'm playing tennis.

They're playing football.

They're going to the zoo.

We're going to a museum.

It's running.

She's going to the library.

1 Match.

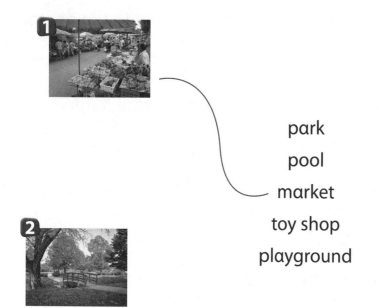

park

pool

market

toy shop

playground

2 Write.

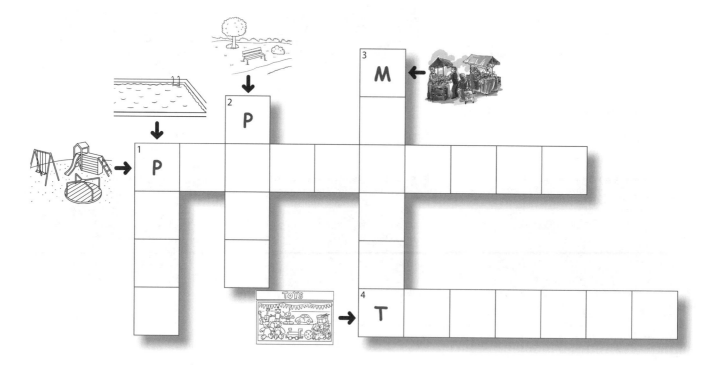

3 Look and tick.

1

Talk! ☐
Don't talk! ✔

3

Go to the park! ☐
Don't go to the park! ☐

5

Sit down! ☐
Stand up! ☐

2

Run! ☐
Don't run! ☐

4

Listen! ☐
Don't listen! ☐

6

Run! ☐
Don't run! ☐

4 Order and write.

1 the guitar! / play / Don't   Don't play the guitar!

2 lose / Don't / the match.   _____

3 the ball! / Kick   _____

4 in the / library. / talk / Don't   _____

5 run! / the lion / Watch   _____

5 Write and draw.

L _ s _ e _ to the lion r _ a _!

ROAR!

1 **Write.**

| drink | eat | ~~have fun~~ | look at | see | take photos |

1

have fun

3

_____

5

_____

2

_____

4

_____

6

_____

2 **Circle and colour.**

1 Let's **look at** / **take photos** of the animals.

2 **Drink** / **Eat** a glass of water!

3 Let's **have fun** / **see** in the park.

4 Look! The penguin **is eating** / **is drinking** a fish!

5 Let's go to the museum and **see** / **have fun** the paintings.

6 Let's **look at** / **take photos** the map.

3 Match.

1 Let's play

2 Let's buy

3 Let's look at

4 Let's have fun

5 Let's watch

6 Let's go

a the paintings in the museum.

b television in the living room.

c football in the park.

d to the swimming pool.

e a toy at the toy shop.

f at the playground.

4 Write.

Look at the giraffes!   Don't take photos.
Let's go to the theatre.   Let's buy a toy!

Let's go to the theatre.

_____

_____

_____

10 Let's Eat!

Lesson 1

1 Look and write.

1 apple / (orange)

3 banana / tomato

5 apple / mango

2 strawberry / tomato

4 banana / mango

6 strawberry / tomato

2 Write.

1 I have got a 🍌 _____banana_____ and an 🍎 _____apple_____ .

2 I have got a _____ and a _____ .

3 I have got an _____ and an _____ .

4 I have got a _____ and a _____ .

5 I have got a _____ and an _____ .

3 Write.

baby	**1**	**babies**	
2		buses	
dress	**3**		
4		boxes	

tomato	**5**		
6		men	
child	**7**		
8		teeth	

4 Count and write.

two feet

_____

_____

_____

_____

_____

5 Read and draw.

1

ten teeth

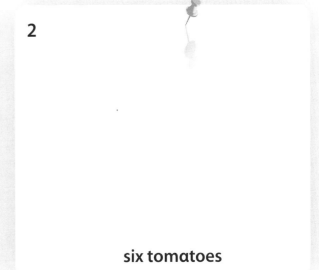

2

six tomatoes

1 **Write.**

1

c <u>h</u> i <u>c</u> k <u>e</u> n

2

c _ e _ s _

3

_ i _ e

4

m _ l _

5

_ r _ a _

6

m _ _ t

7

j _ i _ e

2 **Look. Tick (✔) or cross (✘).**

1 There is some chicken. ✔

2 There is some rice. ☐

3 There is some cheese. ☐

4 There is some bread. ☐

5 There is some juice. ☐

6 There is some milk. ☐

3 Circle.

1 Have you got **any** / **some** bread?

2 We've got **any** / **some** strawberries.

3 I have got **any** / **some** milk.

4 Have you got **any** / **some** bananas?

5 I haven't got **any** / **some** cheese.

6 Dad has got **any** / **some** oranges.

4 Write *some* or *any*.

1 Have we got _____any_____ apples?

2 There are _____ mangoes in the kitchen.

3 I've got _____ cheese.

4 Mark hasn't got _____ rice.

5 Let's buy _____ tomatoes in the market.

6 Are there _____ apples on the tree?

5 Read, Draw and colour.

Let's go to the market
Let's buy some food.
Let's buy five bananas!

Let's go to the market
Let's buy some food.
Let's buy ten tomatoes!

Let's go to the market
Let's buy some food.
Let's buy some bread!

Let's go to the market
Let's buy some food.
Let's buy some meat!

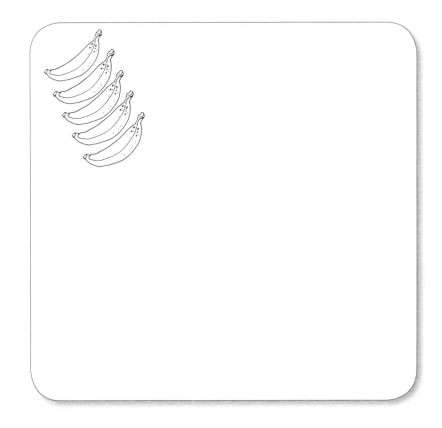

Lesson 3

1 Find, circle and write.

V	E	S	R	A	B	E	J	I	R
T	E	W	N	R	L	I	C	C	B
N	L	E	M	O	N	A	D	E	F
P	O	E	J	E	T	W	N	C	M
R	A	T	C	E	A	P	B	R	R
B	I	S	C	U	I	T	H	E	T
O	Y	E	N	B	R	E	C	A	T
I	L	R	E	V	E	X	B	M	R
C	H	O	C	O	L	A	T	E	L
T	E	M	R	P	E	G	E	H	Y

sweets _____   _____

_____   _____

_____

2 Write.

1 I've got some ___**sweets**___ .

2 Look! There is some _____ .

3  Are there any _____ ?

4 Have you got any _____ ?

5 There isn't any _____ .

3 Circle.

1 Sally is **behind** / **next to** John.

2 The apple is **in** / **on** the table.

3 The red car is **in front of** / **in** the yellow car.

4 The girl is **next to** / **under** the table.

5 The family are **on** / **in** the car.

6 The rabbit is **behind** / **next to** the tree.

4 Write.

in   ~~under~~   on   behind   next to

1 The girl is sitting _____ **under** _____ the apple tree.

2 The bananas are _____ the oranges.

3 The cheese is _____ the table.

4 The man is running _____ the dog.

5 The chicken is _____ the fridge.

5 Read and draw.

There is a book on the table. There are two bananas on the table and an orange next to them. There is a ball on the chair.

81

1 **Find, circle and write.**

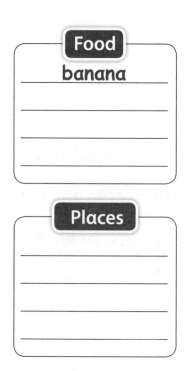

Food
banana
_____
_____
_____

Places
_____
_____
_____
_____

2 **Match and colour.**

1 What are you doing?

2 Where are you going?

3 What is she doing?

4 Where is he going?

5 What is it doing?

6 Where are they going?

a I'm going to the cinema.

b He's going to the toy shop.

c It's eating a banana.

d I'm drinking some milk.

e They're going to the playground.

f She's reading a book in the library.

3 Write and match.

 a

 c

 e

 b

 d

1 eat / ice cream / Let's _Let's eat ice cream._ _____ [d]

2 Let's / some juice / drink _____ [ ]

3 go / to the zoo / Let's _____ [ ]

4 Let's / at the playground / have fun _____ [ ]

5 take photos / Let's/ in the park _____ [ ]

4 Write.

behind   in   in front of   ~~next to~~   on   under

1 Where's the cinema? It's __next to__ the theatre.

2 Where are the children? They're _____ the car.

3 Where's the guitar? It's _____ the chair.

4 Where's the bag? It's _____ the desk.

5 Where's the boy? He's _____ the lion.

6 Where's the rock? It's _____ the boy.

 1
 4
 2
 5
 3
 6

11 Our Wonderful World

Lesson 1

1 Match.

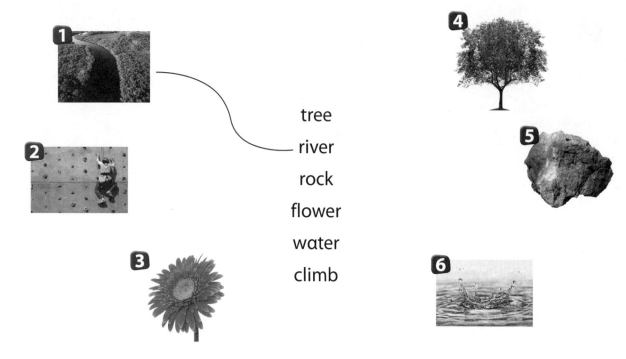

tree

river

rock

flower

water

climb

2 Circle.

1 The boys are swimming in the **rock** / **river**.

2 There are lots of **flowers** / **water** in the park.

3 Can you **climb** / **play** a tree?

4 The cat is in the **tree** / **flower**.

5 There is **water** / **rock** in the river.

6 Is he **climbing** / **running** the rock?

3 Write *like* or *likes*.

1 The girls ____like____ the flowers.

2 I _____ swimming in the river.

3 Sam _____ climbing trees.

4 My dog _____ playing with rocks.

5 You _____ going to the cinema.

6 My brother _____ going to the library.

4 Write.

1 Helen (love) ____loves____ basketball.

2 Mum (go) _____ to the market.

3 The boys (play) _____ football.

4 She (swim) _____ in the river.

5 I (buy) _____ toys at the toy shop.

6 My sisters (like) _____ chocolate.

5 Write and say.

I s **w i m** in the river,

I c _ _ _ _ the trees,

I j _ _ _ over rocks,

It's great!

He g _ _ _ to the park,

He l _ _ _ _ at the flowers.

He d _ _ _ _ _ some water.

It's great!

1 Look and write.

c <u>o</u> l <u>d</u>

__ o __

__ a __ n

s __ __ __ y

__ r __

__ e __

2 Read and write.

1 It isn't h <u>o</u> <u>t</u>. It's c <u>o</u> <u>l</u> <u>d</u>.

2 It isn't w __ __. It's d __ __.

3 It isn't s __ __ __ __. It's r __ __ __ __.

4 The camels are h __ __. They aren't c __ __ __.

3 Write.

1 My sister likes mangoes. She ___doesn't like___ tomatoes.

2 John plays football. He _____ tennis.

3 We run in the park. We _____ in the library.

4 Jane goes to the cinema. She _____ to the theatre.

5 My dad plays the guitar. He _____ the drums.

6 I drink orange juice. I _____ milk.

4 **Look and tick.**

1

Camels climb trees. ☐
Camels don't climb trees. ✔

3

Fish swim in rivers. ☐
Fish don't swim in rivers. ☐

2

We play tennis when
it's rainy. ☐
We don't play tennis
when it's rainy. ☐

4

The children play in the
playground when it's sunny. ☐
The children don't play in the
playground when it's sunny. ☐

5 **Write and say.**

I (not swim) ___don't swim___ in the river when it's cold.

I (not go) _____ to the park when it's wet.

Today is sunny and hot, hooray!

He (not climb) _____ rocks when it's rainy.

He (not take photos) _____ when it's cold.

Today is sunny and hot, hooray!

We (not eat) _____ ice cream when it's wet.

We (not play) _____ in the playground when it's cold.

Today is sunny and hot, hooray!

Lesson 3

1 **Write.**

| spring | ~~summer~~ | autumn | winter |

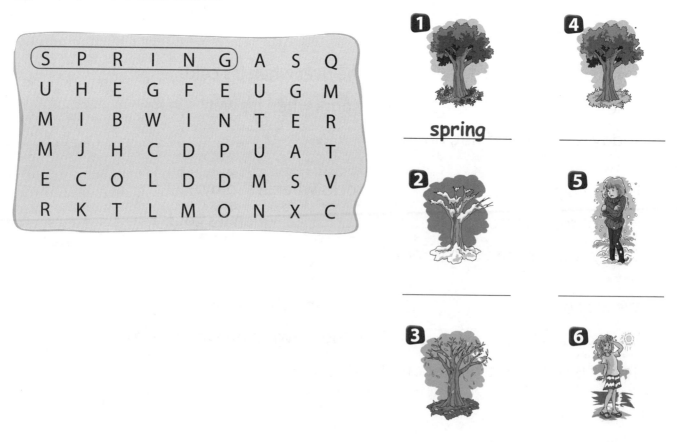

1 summer

3

2

4

2 **Find, circle and write.**

S	P	R	I	N	G	A	S	Q
U	H	E	G	F	E	U	G	M
M	I	B	W	I	N	T	E	R
M	J	H	C	D	P	U	A	T
E	C	O	L	D	D	M	S	V
R	K	T	L	M	O	N	X	C

1 spring

4

2

5

3

6

3 Match.

1 Do you like strawberries?
2 Does your mum swim in the river?
3 Do they play in the park when it's wet?
4 Does your brother like climbing trees?
5 Do you play at the beach in winter?
6 Does the dog like jumping in the sea?

a No, they don't.
b No, we don't.
c Yes, I do.
d Yes, it does.
e No, she doesn't.
f Yes, he does.

4 Write and say.

Helen

George

Mei

Annie

Megan

1 Does Helen like orange juice? _Yes, she does._
2 Does George like climbing? _____
3 Does Mei like swimming? _____
4 Does Annie like reading? _____
5 Does Megan like taking photos of flowers? _____

5 Write about you.

1 Do you like ice cream? _____
2 Does your friend like tomatoes? _____
3 Do you like swimming in the river? _____
4 Does your teacher like apples? _____
5 Do you like it when it's rainy? _____
6 Do you like it when it's cold? _____

12 My Day

Lesson 1

1 Write.

Friday   Monday   Saturday   ~~Sunday~~   Thursday   Tuesday   Wednesday

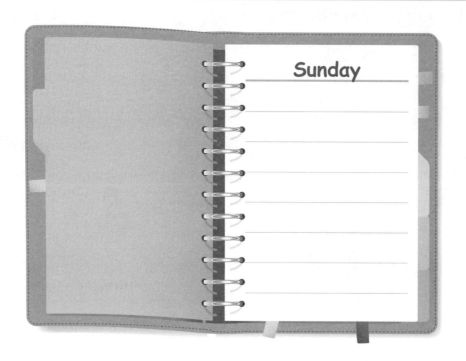

2 Write.

SUNDAY	MONDAY	TUESDAY	WEDNESDAY	THURSDAY	FRIDAY	SATURDAY

1 Sarah takes photos of flowers on ___Saturday___ .

2 Sarah goes to the theatre on _____ .

3 Sarah goes swimming on _____ .

4 Sarah colours pictures on _____ .

5 Sarah eats strawberries on _____ .

6 Sarah plays the piano on _____ .

7 Sarah plays football on _____ .

3 Write *do* or *does*.

1 What ___do___ you do at school?

2 What _____ they do at the park?

3 What _____ he do with the ball?

4 What _____ it do in the water?

5 What _____ Tommy do on Monday?

6 What _____ you do at the weekend?

4 Match.

1 What does your mum do on Tuesday?

2 What do your sisters do at the weekend?

3 What does your brother do on Monday?

4 What do you do on Friday?

5 What does your family do every day?

a They play tennis.

b I play the drums with my friend.

c We go to the market.

d She goes to the library.

e He plays football in the park.

5 Write and say.

S <u>u</u> n <u>d</u> ay is OK.
_ o _ d _ y is OK.
_ u _ s _ a _ is good,
    I say!

W _ d _ e _ d _ y is OK.
_ h _ r _ d _ y is OK.
All the days are good,
    I say.

But Friday is great,
And Saturday is fantastic.
They're the best days,
    I say!

F _ i _ a _ and Saturday.
Friday and _ a _ u _ d _ y.
I love Friday and Saturday!

1 Write.

1 g <u>e</u> t <u>u</u> p

3 _ e _ d _ e _ _ e _

5 h _ v _ b _ e _ k _ a _ t

2 _ a _ e _ u _ c _

4 _ a _ e _ i _ n _ r

6 _ o _ o _ e _

2 Order and colour.

1  ☐

4  ☐

2  ☐ 1

5  ☐

3  ☐

6 ☐

3 Match.

1 Where do you have lunch?

2 What are you doing?

3 What do you do on Monday?

4 Who do you have lunch with?

5 Where do you go on Thursday?

6 Who is that?

a I play the drums.

b My friends.

c I go to the library.

d That's my dad.

e In the dining room at school.

f I'm doing my homework.

4 Circle and match.

1 (Who)/ **What** is that girl?

2 **Who** / **What** is your favourite food?

3 **Where** / **Who** is your school?

4 **What** / **Where** are you doing?

5 **What** / **Where** is your school bag?

6 **Who** / **What** is your favourite sport?

a Chocolate!

b Basketball.

c My sister.

d In my classroom.

e In Cairo.

f Listening to music.

5 Write and say.

breakfast   ~~Get up~~   Go to bed   Who

Get up! Get up!
Sleepy head!
Get up! __Get up__!
What do you do?
You jump out of bed!

Eat your breakfast.
Eat it all!
Eat your _____.
Where do you go?
You go to school!

Run home! Run home!
Let's play a game.
Run home! Run home!
_____ do you play with?
You play with friends!

Go to bed.
_____.
Sleepy head.
What do you do?
You jump into bed!
Good night!

Lesson 3

1 Circle.

at midday /
~~at night~~

in the morning /
in the afternoon

at midday /
at night

in the morning /
in the evening

in the evening /
at night

at midday /
at midnight

2 Write.

1 Do you have breakfast in the  **morning** ?

2 Do you go to bed at _____ ?

3 Does your dad work in the _____ ?

4 Do you have lunch at  _____ ?

5 Do you have dinner in the  _____ ?

6 Do your mum and dad go to bed at _____ ?

3 Write.

one o'clock   two o'clock   ~~four o'clock~~   six o'clock
eight o'clock   nine o'clock   eleven o'clock   twelve o'clock

1 four o'clock

3 _____

5 _____

7 _____

2 _____

4 _____

6 _____

8 _____

4 Circle.

1 (What) / **When** time is it?   It's seven (o'clock) / **midday**.

2 **What** / **When** do you get up?   I get up **at** / **on** six o'clock.

3 **What** / **When** day is it?   It's **midday** / **Monday**.

4 **What** / **When** do you play football?   I play at **the weekend** / **Wednesday**.

5 **What** / **When** do you have lunch?   I have lunch **every day** / **at night**.

6 **What** / **When** do you go to bed?   I go to bed at **morning** / **night**.

5 Write about you.

1 What time do you get up? _____

2 Where do you do your homework? _____

3 Who do you have lunch with? _____

4 When do you go to bed? _____

1 Write.

> autumn   flower   Friday   ~~Monday~~   river   rock
> Saturday   spring   summer   water   Wednesday   winter

Days
Monday
_____
_____
_____

Seasons
_____
_____
_____
_____

Things
_____
_____
_____
_____

2 Write.

do / they / What / do / in the evening?
<u>What do they do in the evening?</u>
<u>They watch TV.</u>

do / they / What / do / on Tuesday?
_____
_____

Nancy / does / do / on Monday? / What
_____
_____

Where / go / Amy / does / every day?
_____
_____

does / What / Harry / do / at the weekend?
_____
_____

at night? / Lily / What / do / does
_____
_____

3 Write.

1 (✔) Kim / play / football.

<u>Kim plays football.</u>

2 (✘) It / be / rainy.

_____

3 (✔) Maria / go to bed / at nine o'clock

_____

4 (✘) Peter / play the drums / in the morning

_____

5 (✘) The children / go to school / in the summer

_____

4 Read and draw.

1
> When do you get up?
> I get up at six o'clock.

2
> When do you have breakfast?
> I have breakfast at eight o'clock.

3
> When do you get dressed?
> I get dressed at seven o'clock.

4
> When do you have lunch?
> I get up at midday.

5 Write about you.

1 What do you do on Monday?

_____

2 Do you like winter?

_____

3 What time do you go to bed?

_____

4 Do you go to the park in the afternoon?

_____

5 Is it sunny today?

_____

My Family

1 **Look at the family tree.**

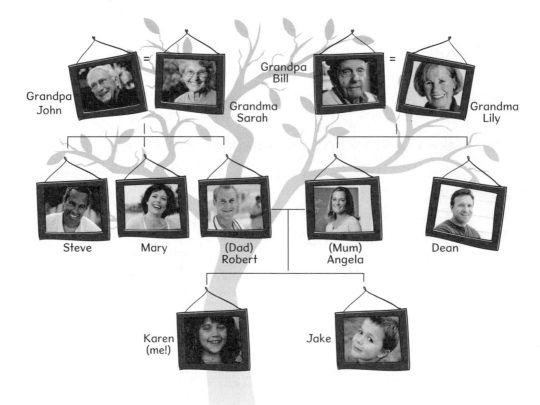

2 **Read what Karen says.**

> Hi! My name's Karen. I'm nine years old. Look! It's my family tree. My family is from Manchester in England. Manchester is cool! My brother is Jake. He's seven years old. My mum is Angela. My dad's name is Robert. I've got two uncles. Uncle Dean is my mum's brother. Uncle Steve is my dad's brother. I've got one aunt, Aunt Mary. She's my dad's sister. I haven't got any cousins. My grandpas are John and Bill and my grandmas are Sarah and Lily. They're old but very funny!

3 **Draw your family tree on a big piece of paper. Draw pictures of everyone, or stick photographs next to their names.**

4 **Write about your family.**

5 **Bring your family tree to school. Show your friends.**

My School

1 **Count and write.**

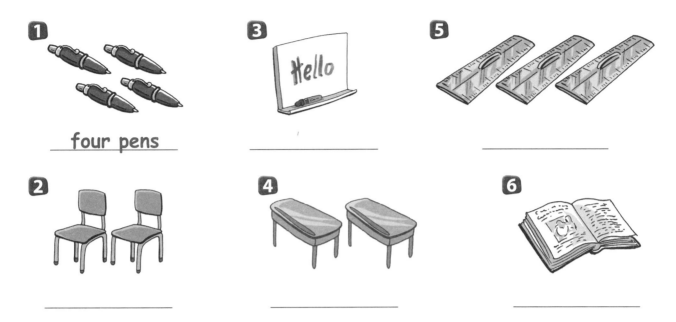

① four pens

③ _____

⑤ _____

② _____

④ _____

⑥ _____

2 **Draw a picture of a classroom on a big piece of paper. Put different numbers of these objects in your picture.**

desk	pencil	teacher
chair	ruler	map
board	book	school bag
pen	rubber	

3 **Bring your picture to school. Work in pairs. Count the items in your partner's picture.**

One teacher! Six desks!

Animals

1 Write.

1

___That___ is a monkey.

3

_____ is an elephant.

5

_____ are turtles.

2

_____ are birds.

4

_____ are whales.

6

_____ is a lion.

2 Make an animal zig-zag book.

1

Cut a piece of A4 paper in half.

3

Stick the sections together.

5

Write 'Animals' on the front.

2

Fold the two pieces into four sections.

4

Fold the strip to make a zig-zag.

6

In each section, draw a different animal. Write its name.

3 Show your zig-zag book to your friends.

My House

1 Look and tick (✔) or cross (✖).

1 Grandma is in the kitchen. ✔

2 Sally is in the bedroom. ☐

3 There is a bird in the garden. ☐

4 Grandpa is in the living room. ☐

5 Dad is in the bedroom. ☐

6 Mum is in the living room. ☐

2 Make a booklet about your house.

Use a piece of A4 paper.

Write 'My House' on the front.

Fold the paper in half.

Draw a different room on each page.
Write a sentence about each room.

3 Show your booklet to your friends.

This is my bedroom. There is a bed and a teddy bear.

1 Write.

feet   legs   eyes   ~~ears~~   mouth   nose   teeth   tail   wing   fin

1. ears
3.
5.
7.
9.
2.
4.
6.
8.
10.

2 Look at this monster. Tell your partner what it's got and what it hasn't got.

It's got three tails. It hasn't got …

3 Draw and colour a big picture of a monster.

4 Bring your picture to school. Work in pairs. Tell your friend about your monster.

It's got six feet. It's got two noses.

My Clothes

1 Write.

> ~~clothes~~ dress jumper shoes skirt socks trousers T-shirt

① clothes

② _____

③ _____

④ _____

⑤ _____

⑥ _____

⑦ _____

⑧ _____

2 Put the words in the box from Activity 1 into the correct columns.

Clothes for girls	Clothes for boys	Clothes for girls and boys
		clothes

3 Draw a picture of yourself in your favourite clothes. Write about them.

> These are my red shoes. I've got a blue T-shirt.

What Can You Do?

1 Write. Answer for you.

Can you _____ **sing** _____ ?
Yes I can _____ .

Can you _____ ?
_____

Can you _____ ?
_____

Can you _____ ?
_____

2 Draw and write four things you *can* do and four things you *can't* do.

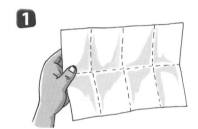

Fold a piece of A4 paper into eight equal parts.

Draw and write what you can and can't do on each piece of paper.

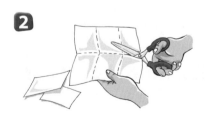

Cut the paper into eight equal parts.

Let's Play!

1 Look at these activities.

> play football   play tennis   play basketball   swim
> play baseball   play hockey   play the piano

2 Write a sentence under each picture.

1

He's playing
baseball.

2

_____

_____

3

_____

_____

4

_____

_____

3 Work in pairs. Choose four different activities from Activity 1.
Practise how to mime them.

4 Work with another pair. Do your mimes. Ask and answer questions.

> Are you playing tennis?

> Yes, we are. / No, we aren't.

5 Change pairs and do the activity again.

My Town

1 Write.

zoo library toy shop museum

Let's go to the zoo!

_____

_____

_____

2 Cut and write.

1  Fold a piece of A4 paper into eight equal parts.

3  Copy the words in the below box onto each piece of paper.

2  Cut the paper into eight equal parts.

park   zoo   toy shop
library   take photos
play football   look at paintings
see elephants

3 Read and say.

Work in pairs. Each keep your words in two piles. Turn them over. Take turns to take one piece of paper from each pile. Make funny sentences.

Let's see elephants in the library!

Let's Eat!

1 Read, draw and colour.

1

There are two bananas next to the apple.

3

There is some chocolate behind the biscuits. There are some strawberries on the ice cream.

2

There is some chicken on the rice. There is some cheese in front of the bread.

4

There are some mangoes on the tree. There are some sweets under the table. There is some lemonade on the table.

2 Draw.

On a big piece of paper, draw and colour the food in your kitchen at home.

3 Bring your drawing to school. Talk about your picture.

We've got some milk. The milk is in the fridge.

Our Wonderful World

1 **Write the names of the four seasons.**

1

spring

3

_____

2

_____

4

_____

2 **Choose a season. Draw and colour a picture of it. Draw you doing an activity.**

3 **Work in pairs. Show your picture to your partner. Ask and answer questions.**

> What season is it?

> What are you doing?

> It's …

> I'm …

PROJECT 12 My Day

1 **Write the days of the week in order.**

> Saturday Friday Monday Thursday Tuesday ~~Sunday~~ Wednesday

1 ___Sunday___   5 _____

2 _____   6 _____

3 _____   7 _____

4 _____

2 **Write about what your friends and family do on different days.**

1 ___My brother plays football___ on Sunday.

2 _____ on Friday evening.

3 _____ every day at seven o'clock.

4 _____ at the weekend.

5 _____ on Monday morning.

3 **Write a diary. Write what you do each day.**

4 **Work in pairs. Ask and answer questions about your diary.**

> What do you do on Friday?

> I play football in the park.

Drawing page

Drawing page

Photo Credits

22(b) Artville; **22(c)** Meta Tools; **34(c)** Corbis; **56(bm)** Epics/Fotolia; **74(br)** Jose Luis Pelaez Inc/Blend Images LLC; **76(tr)** FoodCollection/ StockFood America; **94(tl)** NadyaPhoto/iStockphoto; **96(bl)** Anja Greiner Adam/Fotolia

© Alamy Stock Photo: 31 Jake Lyell/Alamy Stock Photo; **71(tm)** Blickwinkel/Alamy Stock Photo; **77(a)** Kenny/Alamy Stock Photo

© Getty Images: 14; 15 Michael Hevesy/Photodisc; **20(tmb)** JGI/Jamie Grill/Blend Images; **20(b)** Ose Luis Pelaez Inc/Blend Images; **50(a)** Rolleiflextlr/iStock; **52(c)** DoroO/iStock; **56(tl)** Jose Luis Pelaez Inc/Blend Images; **58(d)** Steve Debenport/Vetta; **62(e)** Stockbyte; **64(tm)** Peter Dazeley/Photographer's Choice; **66(tl)** Yukmin/Asia Images; **66(bl)** Tonywestphoto/Corbis Documentary; **70(e)** VisitBritain/ Daniel Bosworth/VisitBritain; **72(d)** Contrastaddict/iStock; **72(e)** Petegar/iStock Unreleased; **75(tl)** Joshblake/E+; **90(a)** Joshblake/E+; **92(br)** Siri Stafford/DigitalVision; **94(bm)** Moisseyev/iStock

© Shutterstock: 16(tl) Wavebreakmedia; **16(bl)** Wavebreakmedia; **16(tr)** Wavebreakmedia; **16(mr)** Wavebreakmedia; **16(br)** Wavebreakmedia; **19** Lucian Coman; **20(t)** Archideaphoto; **20(m)** Taa22; **20(tbm)** All About People; **22(a)** Lotus Studio; **22(d)** 7505811966; **22(e)** Vaclav Krivsky; **24(a)** Irina Nartova; **24(b)** Kucher Serhii; **24(c)** Ijansempoi; **24(d)** Africa Studio; **24(e)** ivn3da; **24(f)** Billion Photos/National Geographic Learning; **25** Monkey Business Images; **27** ESB Professional; **28(t)** Cynoclub; **28(m)** Eric Isselee; **28(rm)** Jiang Hongyan; **28(bl)** Steve Heap; **28(br)** Tanuha2001; **30(tl)** Talvi; **30(bl)** Jaroslava V; **30(bm)** Eric Isselee; **30(tr)** Eric Isselee; **30(br)** Eric Isselee; **32** Joey Danuphol; **33(a)** L. S. Luecke; **33(b)** Joey Danuphol; **33(c)** Konrad Mostert; **33(d)** Rich Carey; **33(e)** VisionDive; **33(f)** Viktor Gladkov; **34(a)** Romakoma; **34(b)** Artazum; **34(d)** Rodenberg Photography; **34(e)** Mashe; **36** Jovana Veljkovic; **38(a)** John Kasawa; **38(b)** 3445128471; **38(c)** Silvano Audisio; **38(d)** Bogdan Florea; **38(e)** Tatik22; **38(f)** J. Helgason; **46(tl)** Darya Prokapalo; **46(ml)** Kokhanchikov; **46(bl)** Kldy; **46(tr)** Sergej Razvodovskij; **46(br)** Charissadescandelotter; **48(a)** Aperturesound; **48(b)** Kedrov; **48(c)** Ta_Ro; **48(d)** Roman Sigaev; **48(e)** Andrej Sv; **50(b)** Roman Sigaev; **50(c)** Vvetc1; **50(d)** Irina Rogova; **50(e)** Andrey Armyagov; **52** Africa Studio; **52(a)** Surrphoto; **52(b)** Surrphoto; **52(d)** Guzel Studio; **52(e)** Chamille White; **54** JIANG HONGYAN; **56(tm)** Pressmaster; **56(tr)** Khakimullin Aleksandr; **56(mtl)** Daxiao Productions; **56(mtm)** Rawpixel.com; **56(mtr)** Andrey Kuzmin; **56(mbl)** MaszaS; **56(mbm)** Sheldunov Andrew; **56(mbr)** Rodolfo Arpia; **56(bl)** Wavebreakmedia; **57** DMHai; **58(a)** Dean Drobot; **58(b)** Africa Studio; **58(c)** Vasily Deyneka; **58(e)** Luis Molinero; **58(f)** Blend Images; **62(a)** Martel; **62(b)** Pukach; **62(c)** Lightspring; **62(d)** Andrey Popov; **64(tl)** Monkey Business Images; **64(tr)** Tammykayphoto; **64(bl)** Pressmaster; **64(bm)** Gino Santa Maria; **64(br)** Anton Lvanov; **66(tm)** RealCG Animation Studio; **66(tr)** Monkey Business Images; **66(br)** RealCG Animation Studio; **70(a)** Ferenc Szelepcsenyi; **70(b)** Kapi Ng; **70(c)** Vereshchagin Dmitry; **70(d)** Nagel Photography; **71(tl)** Wavebreakmedia; **71(tr)** Stefan Nyman; **71(bl)** Fotokostic; **71(bm)** www.hollandfoto.net; **71(br)** Andy Dean Photography; **72(a)** PongMoji; **72(b)** Frida86; **72(c)** Seksan44; **74(tl)** Gpointstudio; **74(tm)** Kotkot32; **74(tr)** Robert Kneschke; **74(bl)** Andrey Popov; **74(bm)** Maxim Ibragimov; **75(tr)** Jurra8; **75(bl)** Michaeljung; **75(br)** Vladi333; **76(tl)** Maks Narodenko; **76(tm)** Tatiana Popova; **76(bl)** Tim UR; **76(bm)** Maks Narodenko; **76(br)** Maks Narodenko; **77(b)** Jocic; **77(c)** SpeedKingz; **77(d)** Vasilyev Alexandr; **77(e)** Viktor Kunz; **77(f)** Syda Productions; **78(a)** Viktor1; **78(b)** Andrey Kuzmin; **78(c)** MaraZe; **78(d)** Azure1; **78(e)** Andersphoto; **78(f)** Joao Virissimo; **78(g)** Nortongo; **80(b)** M. Unal Ozmen; **80(c)** HandmadePictures; **80(d)** Preto Perola; **80(e)** GrigoryL; **84(tl)** Gustavo Frazao; **84(ml)** Carlos Caetano; **84(bl)** Lotus Images; **84(tr)** Majeczka; **84(mr)** Rufous; **84(br)** Serg64; **84** Carlos Caetano; **86(tl)** Andrey Arkusha; **86(tm)** EvgeniiAnd; **86(tr)** Alena Ozerova; **86(bl)** Gornjak; **86(bm)** Sunny Forest; **86(br)** Thaiview; **88(tl)** AlinaMD; **88(bl)** Mny-Jhee; **88(tr)** 1000 Words; **88(br)** Bas Meelker; **89(l)** DenisNata; **89(lm)** Nate Allred; **89(m)** Kenkuza; **89(mr)** InesBazdar; **89(r)** Teresa Kasprzycka; **90(b)** Frescomovie; **90(c)** Renars Jurkovskis; **90(d)** Rob Marmion; **90(e)** Maks Narodenko; **90(f)** Valeri Potapova; **90(g)** Teresa Kasprzycka; **92(tl)** Olesia Bilkei; **92(tm)** Amble Design; **92(tr)** MSPhotographic; **92(bl)** CKP1001; **92(bm)** Svariophoto; **94(tm)** Monkey Business Images; **94(tr)** Rangizzz; **94(bl)** Sirtravelalot; **94(br)** Surachet Meewaew; **96(tr)** Monkey Business Images; **96(mr)** BestPhotoStudio; **96(br)** Jeff Thrower; **96(tl)** MaszaS; **96(ml)** Epiximages; **102(tl)** Christian Musat; **102(bl)** Sebastian Duda; **102(tml)** John Carnemolla; **102(bml)** Alexander Kalina; **102(tm)** Vitor Costa; **102(bm)** Christopher Meder; **102(tmr)** Alexandria Shankweiler; **102(bmr)** Jkitan; **102(tr)** J Reineke; **102(br)** Darya Prokapalo; **104(tl)** Vaclav Hroch; **104(bl)** Jacek Chabraszewski; **104(tr)** Wavebreakmedia; **104(br)** RedBarnStudio; **105(tl)** Tammykayphoto; **105(bl)** Gizmo; **105(tr)** Geo Martinez; **105(br)** Rob Marmion; **106(tl)** Martin Novak; **106(bl)** FamVeld; **106(tr)** Pressmaster; **106(br)** Kapi Ng